# Past Tense
# Future Imperfect
Jon Miller

smith|doorstop

# the poetry business

Published 2023 by
Smith|Doorstop Books
The Poetry Business
Campo House,
54 Campo Lane,
Sheffield S1 2EG

ISBN 978-1-914914-39-3
Typeset by Utter
Printed by People for Print

Smith|Doorstop Books are a member of Inpress:
www.inpressbooks.co.uk

Distributed by NBN International, 1 Deltic Avenue,
Rooksley, Milton Keynes MK13 8LD

The Poetry Business gratefully acknowledges the support of
Arts Council England.

Supported by
ARTS COUNCIL
ENGLAND

# Contents

*for my family*
*with love*

## Eyes

That morning on the beach the first man
to swim round the world arrived back.
No-one was there to greet him – all those
who had waved him off had died, News at Ten,
social media algorithms had all got bored
and moved on and anyway it was assumed
he had drowned in the Sargasso Sea.
Which was a shame because he rode in
on the backs of dolphins, manta rays as
outriders, pale, smooth-skinned, hairless,
having re-grown gills and webbed feet,
barnacles, anemones and bladderwrack
hanging from his back so that when he slopped
unsteadily through the streets of the town
under midnight stars it was as if some creature
from a B movie had come ashore and
that's when the screams began and spread
from house to house and out they came
with flaming torches, billhooks and pitchforks
and drove him back down to the harbour
and into the sea where you can see him
to this day, eyes on the water line but
you will have to imagine his sadness
because like all sea creatures he cannot weep.

## Sound Barrier

My cousin with the sensitive ears
winces as he unbuckles his memory

listens to wallpaper peeling
from his childhood home

hears the aftermath of bats
the pining of snails

and that noise like cellophane crinkling –
his soul wandering the hippocampus

outdoors he wears his astronaut helmet
imagines ambling across a noiseless moon

even on the softest of cushions
sex is drawersful of cutlery crashing from heaven

it is the night he fears most
the way moths boom against his light

stars clink among the hollows of space
bawling at him from a trillion trillion miles

it is this that has led him to make his home
in a deep mine in Yorkshire

where he wishes he could abandon
the body that is his that is thunderstorm

race track marching band and finally
the bombing raid that is his heart.

# *Figures in a Landscape*

They lounge on the last bench down the far end
of Perth Station where the carriages don't reach.

The Girl – cat-slashed jeans, black cat ears, is stuck
like a mollusc to the back of green-haired Biker Boy.

Hard-Faced Friend shouts into the face on her phone,
tugs her peach scrunchy, blows smoke rings emptily.

They pass a can of Strongbow between them,
from time to time pace their cage of sunlight.

Biker Boy kisses diminutive Catgirl
and they sink into their mouths' wet pools –

the musk of cider, spoor of XXX mints
on tongues and come blinking out into the sun

propelled a whole fifteen seconds into the future.
Hard-Faced Friend counts the seagull on the CCTV mast.

Catgirl balances on her heels on the stone rim
of the empty flower bed as if she might fall to her death

three inches below.

# Entomology

They keep coming, the insects,
with parades and fanfares,
mandibles and vomit,
pissing through exoskeletons.

It's me they're after –
antennae frisking the air
like sex pests. Ants conduct
a strip search of my scalp.

Woodlice in battle formation.
A spider in the radar of its web
mummifying its breakfast.
Bedbugs sipping nightcaps of blood.

And legs – millipedes
on their scrolling moustaches.
Caterpillars humping themselves.
Earwigs wielding forceps.

All day this trickle of nibbling,
that underfoot crackle.
I itch like sandpaper
as if my body hair has left me.

As I sleep they hover over me.
Wait to carry me underground
on their million backs to mate
with their queen quivering under the house.

# Shuggie

He's done this for forty years.
Straight out of school
and onto the boats.
All those years in yellow wellies,

those horizons of water
and everything moving beneath him.
The millions of fish whose guts
have spilled over his knife,

his breath in the air in the freezer,
the three men lost overboard,
bobbing briefly then under.
And also the long trail home

down the sea loch to the pier
and into the pub,
the sea still sloshing his walk,
proud of the fight

in his fists planted in the face
of his best mate. And after
the night in the cells,
the phone call to his wife

to pick him up as he falls
into the back seat weeping,
laughing, his yellow wellies
sticking out the side window:

*'Am ah no' yer best man?*
*'Am ah no' yer best man, eh, hen?'*

# A Greek Chorus at the Close of the Tourist Season

This year's crop is on the promenade
Their meat hangs loose under slogans
They amble camel-hoofed in sandals
Their hair ripples in the pastures
They are dazed by tepid pleasures
They sniff the air like blank dogs
They have brought their naked legs
and parade them as Best In Show
Their heartbeats are barely audible
They have eaten of the fruit of the Brainless Tree
They blunder, weightless as helium buffaloes –
we tie them to railings in strong breezes
We cargo them, pack their husks
in ticking rooms of murderous tidiness
We lay them on mattresses that hold
the warmth of octogenarian sex
We plant them on the golf course
We stuff them in wardrobes, stair cupboards
chimneys, sheds, lay them by for winter
We polish our sky each day
We pat our hills into place
We fluff up our forests
Next year we will take their heads
from the shelf, dust them down
rouse them with trumpets, bacon, eggs.

# Nativity

Straw lies about as if someone has detonated a scarecrow.
Miscellaneous barnyard animals position themselves appropriately,
strangely prescient of shopping mall displays across the western world.
A cockerel struts and stares and stares and struts.
Sheep work typewriters in their heads.
The few cows are many tons of bored incomprehension.
Shepherds full of sheep-reek and field-sleep hum
in their hive of odours as if a fank had overflowed.
The Magi examine their cuticles, compose ghazals,
wish for the tiled steam rooms of Jerusalem,
their slaves, their concubines as the rich do everywhere.
Cherubim with bulbous cheeks festoon the rafters,
bob about like party balloons, wearing faces you just want to punch.
Mary in the movie of herself waves her hands over the infant
cleansing the air of some celestial afterbirth with the instinct
of a mother protecting her child from its father.
Joseph leans on his crook, has his doubts.
The world is in a fit of FOMO.
The infant, like all of them, doesn't know what he's started.

# Mayday

We both knew the head's black clag,
the weight swung under the heart, the breath
that couldn't climb the stairs out of our chests.

You'd trained your black lab Mayday to run off,
loved calling it, watching the neighbours panic,
startled from forking the lawn, dead-heading roses.

*Istanbul?* But I had that taxidermy job and you
were glueing your matchstick bust of Rimbaud
to fire up for your Perfect Dinner Party guests –

de Nerval with his lobster and rope,
Mayakovsky loading his pistol,
Woolf soaking wet, Plath reeking of gas.

You checked out that freighter bound for Tuvalu
crewed by Nigerians and Vietnamese, bliss to not know
what they said, not to understand anything for a while

then spent days on Google Earth, turning the planet
till it was nothing but endless Pacific,
atolls floating like dead cells in God's eye.

So ... that day your buzzer didn't work. Blinds down.
Pigeons hungry on your windowsill. Amazon packages
(Estonian poets, Sufi mystics) clogging the storm door.

Even the old woman across the landing who'd hated you
ever since you polka-dotted her shih tzu bit her lip.

When the police unlocked your phone you'd filmed yourself,
naked, junk-shop angels' wings buckled to your back
running the way a child does, full speed, laughing
into the exploding sea, a shroud of surf bursting over you.

*It's a story I tell lonely divorcees late night in bars*
*and bedsits hoping they'll stay, told it*
*so many times I'm not even sure it's true anymore*

*or maybe I'm just filling in my own vague outline,*
*waiting for rescue, firing these flares from the sofa,*
*this lifeboat held out in my palm.*

## Othello

I hadn't picked it up in years and round about
Act III Sc iii was struck by its mechanics.
This wasn't the internal twitching and pinchings
of The Prince or Macbeth's scorpions
contriving their own mismaking; no, this was
Shakespeare's Pompidou Centre – here was
Iago's brazen pipework visible for all to see,
the sheer inevitability of its machinery, pistons
and shafts snaring The Big O in the building
without escape chutes, microlights, anything.

And then on p. 94 – my old student bus pass
(all that hair!) – I must have been reading it
on the way to the hospital and it never struck me
the way it does now – catheters, cannula,
a monitor etchasketching your heart,
morphine drip, colostomy bag, oxygen mask
and there behind your closed lids,
something beating, a moth against the outside light.

# Retail Park

Here is where the city frays at the edges
to low rise warehouses, panting forecourts,
breakers yards, car showrooms, cathedrals of DIY.

On the horizon a parade of glinting towers –
we are far from there in our pallid weekend sun.
Here the compass has failed and we approach

unsure of our bearings among verges,
flags, upper case signage, flailing air puppets,
peering into empty depths of garages and timber yards.

That forklift and cement mixer are archeological,
those stacked pallets home to ants
and not a single fire surround was sold today.

Here the material world, modular, flat-packed.
Here the hot gospellers of the respray,
custodians of filler and stripper, tiles kitchen and carpet.

But watch, as you approach those glass doors,
how they slide apart, steal your reflection
the moment you step inside.

## Lost Child

Not the brazen trumpeters
or the flittering sailboats
or in the minds of mariners
with their white-washed eyes
is there a button of hope.

Neither in the small boys roaming
the fogged avenues
called home for tea
returning with birds' nests
and the ruins of puberty.

You become a twitch
in the fingertips of newscasters
or out here where it happened
the midnight click of the latch
the song in the five-barred gate.

# The Nurses

Here they come
with smirks and instruments
a-glitter on silver trays

down shining corridors
they unhook terrible jaws
to chant hymns and arias

their blouses are full of milk
they have sharks' teeth
and plump plum faces

steady are the hands
that make anagrams
of your inner organs

at night they work out
with coalminers
and lesser Norse gods

or moonlight
as headless mannequins
in department store windows

in their plimsolls
you won't hear them coming
till they shriek

like sirens from ambulances
the wail of your mother
on the day of your birth

# Sir Francis Beaufort Refreshes the Page

1.  Sea lochs placid. Reflections stationary. Small beasts unmolested.

2.  Supermarket trolleys drift. Acid reflux. Newspapers won't fold.
    Body hair rising. Scalps loosen. Extra jersey needed.

3.  Car keys lost. Unfocused rushing about. Conversations out of sync.
    Palindromes only work backwards. Names of grandmothers forgotten.

4.  The way home uncertain. Levitation at street corners.
    Selfies not taken. Ants display subjectivity.

5.  Surge in childhood memories. Subconscious frothing.
    Constant smell of burning. Fruit tastes of detergent.

6.  Children turned inside out. Power lines hum laments and arias.
    Zoos empty. Household dust forms epigrams. Poets give up.

7.  Lesser gods stroll streets and plazas unsurprised. Toddlers pile in
    corners of car parks. Undocumented increase in binge drinking:
    detergent tastes of fruit.

8.  Babies roll across fields. Ravens fuck off. Shouting no longer possible.
    Flags of all nations in tatters. Words all but lost. Bald dogs howl.

9.  Genders interchangeable. Transubstantiation now possible.
    Being a ghost impossible. Self-immolation no longer commented on.

10  Scent of angels burning. Past lives manifest. Pleas for forgiveness abound.
    Roofless churches full. Water reaches weathervanes. Magnetic poles flip.
    Everest Island overpopulated.

11. Sea a mirror. Amphibians re-emerge.

12. Whale song.

# Zorillo (Skunk Song)

we is not the dogs of Jupiter and pinkie lift
      is not sequinned dreams of queens
          of May and prom

we is piss fox in us stink caps
      we is wet nurse to your infants
          us lipsticky mouths abuzz of honeybees

we mace sulphurous we is artists
      we basquiat we banksy we tag we spray
          we hose we dub end-to-end your yards and palaces

we is indelible we pheromone arsonists
      perfumiers of Skunk Kiss reeking
          of the underside of your mistress

                        come closer

      worship our arses
our punky cunts

# One Day I'm Gonna Take the Kids to Disneyworld

Down at the No-Star Motel the transients are hollering toothless hallelujahs and setting off bottle rockets to fire up the desert sky this Thanksgiving night while on the sofas in the parking lot, addicts sparked out on meth and crack happily hopeless glaze face down among stuffed animals and Disney pillows as the chihuahua on the lilo in the pool yaps for treats and dry land at the random naked people screaming at their kids to *get to fuckin sleep* an imprecation which includes the fourteen year old livewire firing the dumpster to rhapsodise his love for the soon-to-be-married seventeen year-old covered in tattoos of old boyfriends who is busy self-harming in order to attract the attention of the oiled Mexican in his Speedos doing pull ups in his doorway and

all the while down at reception strung with fairy lights and a flashing neon Jesus, the Pentecostal couple who run the place are putting the finishing touches to their mural of THE RAPTURE – tiny figures shooting up out of the motel on their way to meet The Lord, soaring past planes tumbling out of the sky as their pilots are called and the cockpits empty and the planes fall like bottle rockets to rejoin the rest of its precious flailing cargo busy figuring out how to escape the gravity of another day on earth.

## They Made A Crime Series Here

We are miles off Hringvegur, American satnav garbling
*'Fjardarheidi'*: a high pass, a blizzard shreds the windscreen,

then down to Seydisfjordur, where the road stubs itself out
against the fjord; like us, it has given up fighting the inevitable.

Past the fish factory, its yellow flag cracking the wind.
Corrugated sheds, oil tanks. Houses stare into themselves.

This town has let out all its breath, waits to take another
next century. For the lonely, binoculars stand on windowsills.

A thought bubble: *Stay low. The world is not your lobster.
Tie everything down. Run for port. A beard hides a lot of guilt.*

Picnic benches crouch like crabs at car parks and supermarkets;
husbands keep engines running in case wives make a break for it.

A camper van – rented – drifts by, turns down the wrong road,
bikes shrouded in grey, a child's face at the window.

Beside the filling station three farmers lean into a trailer,
debate the efficacy of bladed implements. One looks up.

Nothing connects until everything does. We have tickets,
drive into the ferry, its belly, its deep machine hum, extras no longer.

# Marseille, it was winter

Beyond the cafe under the arcades, night closed in,
tobacco, pastis, the harbour on its breath.
Snow on the lions guarding the emperor's statue
and on the horses waiting for centuries by their carriages.

Above the young couple reeled ceiling fans
and from time to time the bell over the door jangled.
On their plates, the shattered remains of mussels
quails' eggs, pigeon breast, pomegranates

as if they might discover some oracle in shells,
the organs of birds and beasts. She spoke
at all times using implements – lipstick, fork,
salt cellar, cigarette case – for illustration

and a sadness tumbled through her words
as if swans were falling from the sky she could not catch
while his hands moved over the tablecloth
straightening cutlery, fingertips reading the crumbs

as he wondered over which mountain range
he would have to make his way to finally forget her.
And when she left, without her coat, her scent fluttered
between our tables and I ran with him as he poured himself

into the emptiness of her chair.

# Sniper

In the street, tanks, rubble.
Soldiers wear patterns of sand.
The village a jigsaw of dust.
Children in doorways hold the hands of ghosts.
I sight along the muzzle buried in a hole in the air.
You are small, distant. The size of a sparrow. Smaller.
You have no family. Were never born.
You are just a single dot of God.
I crouch behind chimneys. Aerials. Satellite dishes.
I watch the wind in the flags.
I take small cups of breath.
My heart hibernates. I am almost dead.
With my one eye, I come at you out of nothing.

# Memory Moth

Drawn on by memory's moth, I pedal the back lanes,
and tree-lined avenues, the dim suburban parks,
handlebars dusted with childhood.

Tyres whisper Beechwood, Woodcroft, Broomhill,
as my reflection slips over polished bonnets,
shimmers under streetlights, just me and my sodium ghost.

I know no-one here now, the sons and daughters
I ran with misplaced, the past falling
behind hedgerows, curtained windows, bland driveways.

And there you are, kicking a ball down the far end
of an endless evening, night gathering in the goal posts,
a running boy who hasn't happened yet;

or stood stock still having run right into himself,
only to vanish. We are somewhere and nowhere
as we have always been.

# The Moon is Moving Away from the Earth at 3.78 Centimetres A Year

So gradually as darkness stretches
wolves will forget their birchwood howl
and lunatics speak in perfectly comprehensible sentences.
Werewolves will apply for Civi List pensions,
vampires for Council preservation grants.
Numbered footnotes in poems will explain
its appearance, orbit, its romantic silveriness, etc.
*Fly Me to the Moon, Bad Moon Rising,*
*Dark Side of the Moon, Moon River,*
*Blue Moon of Kentucky* like Mongolian throat singing
or Gregorian plainsong will only be performed
by enthusiasts in cloisters and cathedrals
on feast days and holy days.
*Moon* will go the way of words like
*brephophagist, welmish* and *weequashing*
Frogs will no longer have a froggy sex life
and pearl necklaces will vanish from necks.
Some philanthropist will build a Moon Museum
with information boards, interactive Moon apps,
touchscreens, 3D VR headsets to watch it
sail through the sky, your goggles filling with tears.
Tides will cease, seaweed shrink, the earth stagger,
and in the motionless seas sharks will halt,
sink headfirst to the ocean floor.

# As a Child She Played With Her Hands, Her Only Pets

And, Jennifer, who told you you were beautiful?
You were plain, a spaniel's brown hair
your thoughts pale as wheat
your heart beating a high and lonely piccolo.

Who held you close as a starfish?
Who called for you in the night
or knitted you something shapeless?

They pulled you from the sea and gave you to the nuns
filled your hands with hymnals, made mirrors of abstraction.

Each night, God's erection rose under your single sheet
and you held on for dear life.

Woodland creatures come to my door to ask after you.
Sparrows leave messages in bottles wishing you happy birthday.
No, they don't. Of course they don't. Never have.

Some days I stand stock still among perfumes of department stores.
I throw a stick for my dog but it keeps bringing it back.

Other days, I stop lifts between floors and wait for rescue.

# *Left Alone It Will Spin*

Keep to the forgotten parts of forests.
Keep lichen-side of birches,
rooting fossils and scut, holt and sett,
lantern-lit, hardwired to constellations.

Avoid the wagons and thin plumes of smoke,
village guards, look-out towers, barking dogs.
Whittle arrows for your quiver as you walk.
Your child will not look at you and sleeps fearfully.

✳ ✳

Keep a medieval silence out beyond the last smoking city,
the last beached whale, crowded islands with their rising waters.

✳ ✳

Up there in the trees, the crashed astronaut.
His white suit, a punctured chrysalis.
His golden visor, his one golden eye,
for a moment held blue marbled beauty,
his last utterances, ghost signals,
white noise hung in the branches.

✳ ✳

Put on the visor.
Walk golden-eyed through the ruins
on the last breath of a planet.

# This Way to the Observation Lounge

Out through the placid archipelagos they go
at ease in their daylit aquarium
moving over water at the pace of a slow car.

The sea is flat on its back. The flag barely mutters
at the mast. All are hypnotised by empty sea and sky,
by the line where nothing meets.

They have left the world to turn without them.
and sit with hands clasped in laps
as if listening to a sermon on vacancy.

Asleep, they twitch to escape their clothes.
They know themselves the way the blind
feel what they cannot see.

I could tuck in chins, settle a head on its neck,
retrieve dropped novels, while their eyes read dreams
the way an unborn child pushes against its mother's belly.

They are at rest. Someone is on the bridge.
Over the horizon is harbour. Weather is busy somewhere else.
Who they are has fallen away like rain over islands.

# Acknowledgements

Thanks are due to the editors of the following publications in which some of these poems first appeared: *The North*, *Strix*, and *Dreich* sometimes in a slightly different form. 'Sniper' was shortlisted for the Wigtown Poetry Prize 2021.

I would also like to acknowledge my deep gratitude to Peter Sansom for his gentle yet scrupulous guidance and encouragement in considering these poems but also to Ann and all involved in doing invaluable work at The Poetry Business.

Thanks to Donny O'Rourke for his expansive consideration of several of these poems that also went under the scrutiny of his poetry group and came out relatively unscathed.

And as always, for everything, to Lesley.